A
DINOSAUR
at the
BUS STOP

For Hamish – K.W.
For Ruaridh, Struan, Lachie
and Callan – E.M.

Text copyright © Kate Wakeling 2023
Illustrations copyright © Eilidh Muldoon 2023

First published in Great Britain
and in the USA in 2023 by
Otter-Barry Books, Little Orchard,
Burley Gate, Herefordshire, HR1 3QS
www.otterbarrybooks.com

A catalogue record for this book is available
from the British Library
Designed by Arianna Osti

ISBN 978-1-91307-420-3
Illustrated with pen and ink and digital media

Printed in the UK by Clays Ltd.

9 8 7 6 5 4 3 2 1

MIX
Paper from
responsible sources
FSC® C018072
FSC
www.fsc.org

A DINOSAUR at the BUS STOP

POEMS TO HAVE FUN WITH!

By Kate Wakeling

Illustrated By Eilidh Muldoon

Otter-Barry BOOKS

Contents

Cloud Stories

Tell me,
what do you spy
in that big old sky?

What pictures
what people
what faces
what places
what ships
what shapes
what cats
what bats
what five-legged pigs wearing very tall hats
do you see?

Tell me,
why do I see a shoe
where you see a canoe?

And why do you see a tree
where I see a chimpanzee?

The clouds are telling tales
up up in the blue.

A story for me,
a story for you.

Mr Long Gets Everything Wrong

Mr Long gets everything wrong.

He wears socks on his head,
he eats jelly in bed,
and spreads the silvery slime
of a snail on his bread.

Yes, Mr Long gets everything wrong.

He cleans his teeth with a spoon,
thinks he was born on the moon,
and when everyone's sleeping
sings VERY LOUD tunes.

Oh, Mr Long gets everything wrong.

He plays the drums with his nose,
eats noodles with his toes,
and sunbathes in his underpants
all day when it snows.

But perhaps Mr Long doesn't get
everything wrong.

For when all's said and done
I think he might
have a lot more fun
than someone who gets everything

right.

9

Probably the Fastest Poem in the World

(To be read as quickly as you dare.)

Lightning bolts and racing cars
and laser beams and shooting stars,

bullet trains and bats and cheetahs,
the world-record holder for the 100 metres,

faster faster, don't get slow,
faster faster, go go go,

tadpoles, drum rolls, winning goals,
feet tiptoeing across hot coals,

water slides and jumbo jets,
the cat on hearing it's time for the vet's,

faster faster, don't get slow,
faster faster, go go go,

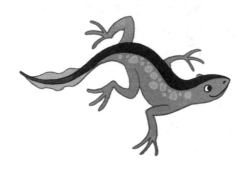

a newt (they're faster than you think),
a kangaroo, a sneeze, a blink,

the speed of sound, the speed of light,
the speed of ketchup when your T-shirt's
white,

faster faster, don't get slow,
faster faster, go go go,

all the things that whizz and zoom
and zip and zap and whoosh and vroom

and sprint and scurry in top gear,
um, is that *steam* coming out your ear?

(Best we stop this poem here.)

How to Bob Like a Robin

(*Please* do *try this at home.*)

hop to the right
(light as a feather)

hop to the

left

on the spot: hop hop hop

nod

nod
nod

BLINK

then think   *hard*   about

worms

jiggle tail feathers
quick!
wiggle foot

tip head one way

tip head other way

stay
still

look up to the
sky

open your wings

and

FLY

Splinter

Tiny splinter
in my foot,

bit of wood that's
staying put.

I don't know
how it got in

but it's stuck
beneath my skin.

Cuts and scrapes,
a graze, a bruise:

all of these
I'd rather choose

than this tiny
scrap of tree

that is lurking
inside me.

Someone, won't you
tell me how

a thing this small feels
quite so OW?

Rain

but oh the rain has such small hands
fingertips tapping on the window-pane
pattering *hello hello hello*
to the boy in his bed
to the cat being fed
to the moon and owl and worm and crow

and oh the rain has such small feet
that tiptoe softly down the street
and dance on the bus stop
and dance on the grass
and dance on the roofs with a light quick beat

and oh the rain has a big big heart
that does its part
and turns the world to brightest green
and washes it clean
and fills the puddles on cold grey days
so you, yes you, can jump and splash and play
and play and play

*Some of this poem sprang to life from a line by
the poet E. E. Cummings: 'not even the rain has such
small hands'.*

Skeleton Pete

When the sky is all dark
and the day is all done,
then Skeleton Pete
wakes up for some fun.

He's a rickety-clickety
bundle of bones,
he munches on eggshells
and juggles with stones.

He's thin as a lamp post,
he's quick as a sneeze,
(he can make very interesting
sounds with his knees).

He cheers up the cats
with his skeleton tunes,
then rattles his elbows
and grins at the moon.

And yes, he's a strange one,
an odd-looking thing:
He hasn't a tummy,
or hairs on his chin.

But he dances along
to his skeleton beat
and he knows who he is
from his skull to his feet,
and (I *think*) that he's someone
who I'd like to meet:
he's rickety-clickety
Skeleton Pete.

The Pudding Place

When you're full of food,
when you're crammed
with scrambled eggs
or chicken legs
or rice and peas
or macaroni cheese,
and all you can say is:
please please *please*
don't make me eat another bite –

well, do you find
if someone brings out
something sweet,
a tasty treat
like pancakes oozing with syrupy yum
then, suddenly,
BOOM,
inside your tum
you've room?

I call this space
the pudding place.

Because even the fullest belly
is ready
for raspberry jelly.

And grownups say:
no no *no*,
you didn't eat your beans,
you can't have room for this
ice cream.

But it's true:
you *do* have space
at the end of a meal,

because
the pudding place is real.

In the Quiet of the Trees

Shrin yoku *is an idea in Japan which means 'forest bathing', or enjoying the calm and quiet of being in a forest.*

The forest is a special kind of still.

In the quiet of the trees,
I breathe deep as roots.

My mood grows as bright
as the light
that streams through leaves.

My thoughts open like buds.

I let my worries rest on softest moss.

The forest is a special kind of still

and in the quiet of the trees
I become
a special kind of me.

Kite Day

pull

for kite flight

time's right

I spy

breeze in trees

I spy

fly

how you make my brain
sky high
bright kite

WHOOSH
swoosh

string tight

push

The Monster Jamboree

On Saturdays at half past three,
the monsters have their jamboree.

They come from near and far away
to stomp and sing and howl and play.

They fill their tums with monster snacks
(their favourite treat is troll earwax),

then put on special monster hats,
made of socks and twigs and bats.

Next, they play their monster games,
which often end in fights and flames

but monsters do not mind this stuff
(and those that do wear large ear muffs),

and when at last the clock strikes eight
the monsters know it's getting late.

They sadly shake their monster heads
and stomp home to their messy beds

to dream their sweetest monster dreams
of next week's monster jamboree.

A Dinosaur at the Bus Stop

What if
you were at the bus stop,
looking at the sky,
and a dinosaur plodded by?

Sure, we all know
the dinosaurs dropped dead
years ago.

But what if
instead
they were still around today?

Would they look at us
(*gulp*)
like we were lunch?

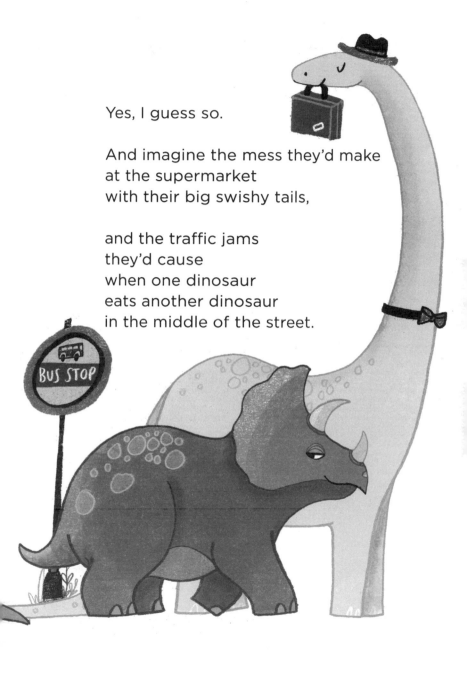

Yes, I guess so.

And imagine the mess they'd make
at the supermarket
with their big swishy tails,

and the traffic jams
they'd cause
when one dinosaur
eats another dinosaur
in the middle of the street.

But maybe sometimes
they'd be fun?
The fast little feathery ones
could be good to play football with.

And if there was a splashy dinosaur
at the swimming pool,
things could get exciting.

Would we keep them as pets?

Or
(*gulp*)
would they keep *us* as pets?

OK, fine,
it's good news
the dinosaurs are all gone

...if they definitely are?

It's true I've never seen one,
but when you're next at the bus stop,
I'd keep an eye

just in case

a dinosaur

plods by.

My Home

My home has an interesting secret:
my home knows all sorts about me.
It knows when I laugh and it knows when I cry
and it knows what I like for my tea.

My home knows my favourite story.
My home knows the toy I like best.
It knows when I pick at my toenails
and it knows if I put on my vest.

My home knows what I find most funny.
It knows when I'm cross or fed up.
It knows when I'm lost in a daydream
and it knows why I don't like *that* cup.

Yes, my home has an interesting secret
and if there was some sort of a test
that asked what I'm like,
what I do, who I am,

well, my home is who knows me the best.

Ready Steady Steam Train

(Here is a poem to start off reading as slowly as possible, then gradually get faster and faster as the train gets going.)

Here is the station
and here is the train,

polished and waiting
to travel again.

The coal has been shovelled,
the fire is now lit,

the flames start to crackle
and spatter and spit.

The water is boiling,
the steam starts to push,

and off goes the train
with a squeal and a whoosh,

and the engine goes hiss
and the carriages sway

and faster and faster,
the train moves away

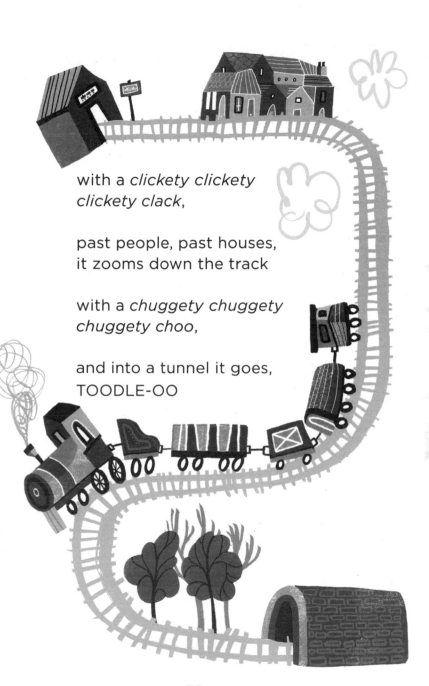

with a *clickety clickety clickety clack*,

past people, past houses, it zooms down the track

with a *chuggety chuggety chuggety choo*,

and into a tunnel it goes, TOODLE-OO

The Wind is in a Big Bad Mood

The wind is in a big bad mood today.

There it goes,
rushing about,
throwing things in the air
and making a fuss.

It howls at the windows,
and scowls at the trees
till they get so upset
they drop their leaves.

This morning
I watched that big bad wind
shove a cloud
right across the sky.

And get this:
when I went outside,
it even pulled my hair.

I suppose
stuff like waves and kites and windmills
are thrilled the wind is in a huff.

But it's quite enough
for me
so I'm not going to thank it.

Nope, I'm staying safe inside,
tucked under this blanket.

Five Mini-Beast Riddles

1.
pink wriggler
thick as a finger
soil breather
mud muncher
earth scruncher

2.
ground slurper
house heaver
trail leaver
foot slimer
slow timer

3.
happy to wait
4 + 4 = 8
silk spinner
(fly for dinner)

4.
tiny toe tickler
egg layer
team player
root creeper
hill heaper

5.
often hairy
(sometimes scary)
egg hatcher
leaf attacher
butterfly beginner

1. worm   2. snail   3. spider   4. ant   5. caterpillar

Me and the Dark and the Wardrobe Door

When I'm in bed
and out goes the light,
well, sometimes the things in my room
seem to *change*
at night.

I look and I look
and I'm sure
the wardrobe door
is a creature with
claws.

And the bookcase
grows a
spooky face.

And that pile of clothes
becomes a crocodile
with a horrible
smile.

So I shout out
and in you come
and on goes the light
and *whoosh*
everything's alright.

And I know
it's just my brain
playing tricks.

There are no monsters
or meanies here.

No witches on broomsticks.

But when we switch off the light
and once more
it's me
and the dark
and the wardrobe door,

this time,
I keep my eyes
shut
tight.

My Treasures

These are treasures that I keep,
I hold them close before I sleep.

A silver coin,
a twisty shell,
a leaf that has a lovely smell,

a birthday badge,
an apple pip,
a very shiny paperclip,

an acorn cup,
a curly straw,
the key to a forgotten door.

These are treasures that I found.
I keep them safe,
I keep them sound.

Sad Song

Sometimes a sad song sings through me.

Nobody else can hear it.

The sad song hums round my head,

    thumps its beat deep in my tummy,

      strums a sigh from my lungs.

Sometimes the sad song stays too long,
gets stuck,
gets loud.

So, when I can't change my tune

or reach its end,

I sometimes sing my song to a friend

and find

a bright new song begins.

Pick a Sound, Any Sound

What's your favourite noise?
What's the best sound around?

What would you choose
from all the world's whoops
and fizzes
and gurgles
and BOOMS?

A space rocket zoom
or popping balloons?

Tiger sneezes
or seaside breezes?

A brilliant burp,
the honk of a goose,
or the *slurp* of your straw with one last sip
    of juice?

It *could* be the crunch of a cornflake
    mid-munch.

Or
are yours
the sort
of ears
to cheer
the soft-as-silk sounds?

The swoosh of a cloud,
the shush of a secret,
the creak of trees,
hum of bees,
swish of a grasshopper rattling its knees.

Or even the hush that hangs when everything
STOPS.

Listen.

So what do you think?
What's the best sound around?
A raindrop's *plink,*
an ocean's roars,
a hippo's snores?

The choice (of course) is yours.

A Very Serious and Important Dance

Jump up in the air
like you're a startled kangaroo,
shake a foot around
like there's a stone inside your shoe,

crouch down to the ground
and lay a dinosaur egg,
squirm as if a baby squirrel's
climbing up your trouser-leg,

wobble wobble wobble
like a human bowl of jelly,
play the drums like mad
with just your hands and just your belly,

puff out both your cheeks
like you're a hamster eating toast,
blink three times in shock
as if you think you've seen a ghost,

swirl your arms around you
like a squid amid the ocean,
stamp stamp stamp your feet
to make a thundery commotion.

And now the dance is done: top work,
three cheers, thumbs up, kapow,
the only thing that's left for you
to do is take a bow.

Hamsters, Sharks and Life on Mars

Aisha likes to rollerskate,
Mo likes baking cakes,
Jia likes to look at books
of spiders, sharks and snakes.

Tess likes trampolining,
Luke likes kangaroos,
Imran likes to stomp around
in sparkly silver shoes.

Different brains like different stuff
to think about and do:
it could be maps and tap-dancing,
or hamsters and kung fu.

Ali likes to sing along
to songs with loud guitars,
Jim (who lives next door) prefers
to dream of life on Mars.

Basma's into robots,
Alina likes to knit,
Dot likes drawing jellyfish
while in her football kit.

Yes, different brains like different stuff
to think about and do,
and what it is that *your* brain likes,
well, that bit's up to you.

My Stick Collection

My stick collection
is the best on our street.

It's the pick
of the park's sticks.

It's perfection,
this collection.

Straight,
knobbly,
big,
small,
thin,
thick:
my stick collection's got it all.

I can't say
what makes a certain stick
just right
for the pile.

But I know one
when I see one.

And I can't say
when this collection
will be complete.

But I know this:
my stick collection
is the best on our street.

If I Was an Ant

If I was an ant,
your shoe
would be
(to me)
the size of a ship.

And if I was an ant,
that chair
over there
would feel like a
skyscraper.

If I was an ant
walking over your dinner plate,
that dollop of tomato ketchup
would be a sticky red lake
and that chip
would feel like a golden bridge
to a world beyond.

And if I was an ant
this poem
would take a
very
very
very
long time to read.

Eleven People on the Bus

On the bus, the people sit,
some pick their nose,
some chat, some knit.

1 is dreaming of the sea,
2 is wondering what's for tea,

3 is scared they'll miss their stop,
4 just wants a lollipop,

5 sings 6 a lullaby,
7 swats a buzzy fly,

8 talks loudly on the phone,
(9 now wishes they'd walked home),

10 is tired with far to go,
11 has an itchy toe.

Eleven people on their way,
through eleven sorts of day.

This is a Sensible Fart Poem*

This is a sensible fart poem
because there's nothing funny about farts.

You wouldn't be the sort of person
to find a fart funny,
would you?

Of course not.

And we can all agree
that what *isn't* funny about farts
is the noise they make.

The way they slide out with a little hiss.

Or thunder round the room
with a squelch.

There is nothing funny about this.

And then there's the smell of farts.
The eggy stink of a really large fart.

Also: not funny.

Why would a gust of gas
squirting out of a bottom
make anyone smile?

Because the funny things in this life
are jokes
and clowns
and people falling over on banana skins.

Not farts.

Not a guff
or a trump
or a pump
or a bottom burp
or a little tommy squeaker.

Nope, there's nothing funny about farts,
is there?

** This is a very sensible poem. It is important that
anyone reading or listening to this poem stays
very serious and very sensible from beginning to
end. Thank you.*

59

Edna the Tremendous

Meet Edna the Tremendous,
she truly is the best,
she rides a flying bicycle
and wears a stripy vest.

She eats ice cream for breakfast
(her favourite's mint choc chip),
then zooms off catching baddies
with just her fingertip.

She's fiercer than a tiger,
she's braver than a bear,
she tells the truth, is kind to slugs,
and has bright purple hair.

She keeps a pet flamingo,
her burps are loud as rockets,
she always has some jam on toast
stored in her trouser pockets.

Sharks or monsters, trolls or meanies:
Edna will defend us.
She's big, she's bold, she's solid gold,
she's Edna the Tremendous.

The Washing Machine Jive

In the washing machine jive
see your clothes come alive,
watch them bounce, watch them whizz
as those soap bubbles fizz.

See your trousers start whirling,
and your T-shirts go twirling,
hear your jumper and jacket
make a marvellous racket.

Your pyjamas are bopping,
your socks can't stop hopping,
your T-shirts are wriggling,
and your pants? Yep, they're jiggling.

So please pull up a chair,
as the things that you wear
start to skip, dip and dive,
start to bubble alive,
let's all give a high five
for the washing machine jive.

My Cold

(For best results, I suggest reading this poem aloud while also pinching your nose. Unless you already have a cold, in which case this poem was MADE FOR YOU.)

I've got this cold
and it's terrible.

First, I had a tickle
in my throat.

Then came a trickle
of gunge
out my left nostril.

And now
I'm so bunged up
I may as well not *have* a nose.

You could put
ten especially stinking toes
right next to my face
and I wouldn't smell a thing.

At breakfast today
Mum asked why I wasn't being more
polite
and I said:
when you're full of sneezes
it's hard to remember your thank yous
and pleases.

So she held out a tissue and
said BLOW.

And I said no.

Because it's *my* cold
and I'll sniff if I want to.

Five Ocean Riddles

1.
big biter
wave slicer
fin carrier
fish worrier
ocean warrior

2.
tentacle dancer
(8 is the answer)
expert thinker
ink squirter

3.
green shelled
flipper flapper
mouth snapper
air sipper
head tucker

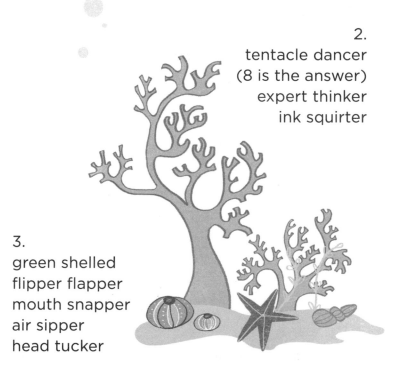

4.
big as a bus
ocean crosser
tail swisher
sea singer
blowhole whoosher

5.
little nipper
food gripper
sideways stepper
sand creeper
shell keeper

The Fire of London Town

City of wood,
summer of heat:

big bad luck
when these two meet.

Pudding Lane,
midnight dark,

baker's oven,
jumping spark.

Something's burning
(it's not bread),

quick as lightning,
fire has spread.

East wind blows
and fire roars,

gobbling roofs
and walls and doors.

Four long days
the flames burn hot,

stealing all
that London's got.

Four long days
of burning down:

this is the fire
of London town.

After a long dry summer, the Great Fire of London swept through the city in September 1666. The fire began in a bakery on Pudding Lane then burnt on for four days, destroying much of the old city of London.

The Splendid Song of the Bat, the Rat, the Dolphin, the Hippopotamus, the Rhinoceros, the Sloth and the Tiger*

*All these animals make noises (some very high and some very low) that the human ear, alas, can't hear.

My New Pet

My new pet
is a funny sort of animal.

He has the body of a little horse,
so I can ride on his back
and sure, it's a bit of a squeeze,
but he can just about snooze
at the end of my bed.

He has the legs of a kangaroo
so is great at hopping
and, with his zebra stripes,
I can always spot him.

His fur is velvety as a bear's
(which makes my pet oh so soft to pat)
and instead of a nose,
he has a neat little elephant's trunk
which makes bath time
terrific.

Tucked at his sides
are two huge eagle's wings,
so when we get bored
we take a spin through the clouds.

Yes, my new pet
is a funny sort of animal,
it's true.

So get set,
because if *you* could dream up
a new sort of pet,
what kind of creature
would you choose?

An Odd Problem

Tell me,
if I kept my socks
in a box
with seventeen locks
and some really big rocks
on top,
would this stop
some of my socks
hopping off
to wherever it is
socks
go?

(The answer,
of course,
is no.)

The Interesting Thing About Yawns

is you can give them like a gift

or pass one round a room
like a bowl of crisps.

Here I am,
yawning with a mouth like a fish

[insert an enormous yawn here]

and the next thing you know,
everyone nearby is yawning too.

That said,
even if you *can*,
it turns out no one thinks it very pleasant
if you give them a yawn for their
birthday present.

The Names I Give My Toes*

1. Tiny Tara

2. Wilbur the Wonky

3. Mr Medium

4. Fancy Fiona (who wishes she was a finger)

5. Big Angry Bob

6. Charlie the Chunk

7. Ninja Nancy

8. Giggles McWiggles

9. Captain Sleepy

10. QUEEN KALINKA THE TINY BUT MIGHTY ALL-POWERFUL RULER OF FEET

* What do you call yours?

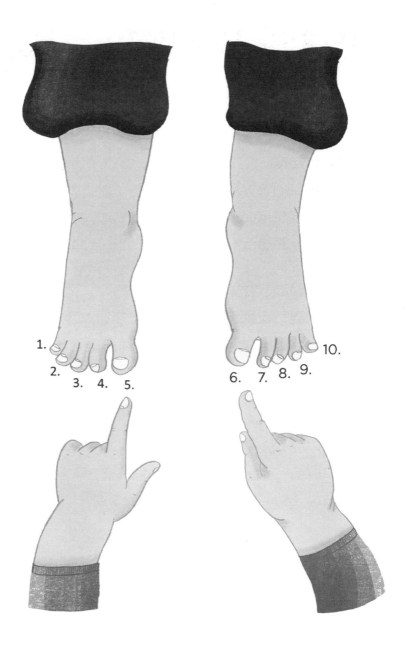

1.
2.
3. 4. 5.

10.
6. 7. 8. 9.

Sky Music

The sky is filled with music.

The sun wakes up
to pluck
a gold guitar.

The clouds huff and puff.
They toot on flutes.

An aeroplane swoops by
and tap-tap-taps the drum of the sky.

Then comes night.

The stars ring tiny bells of light,
ting-a-ling-a-ling-a-ling.

The moon sings
his soft, sweet tune:
sleep tight sleep tight sleep tight

And the sky
        begins
                to
                        snore.

© Sophie Davidson

KATE WAKELING

grew up in Yorkshire and Birmingham. Her first collection of children's poems, *Moon Juice*, won the CLiPPA Prize in 2017 and was nominated for the Carnegie Medal. Her second, *Cloud Soup*, was a Book of the Month in the Guardian and the Scotsman and shortlisted for the CLiPPA. Kate has performed her poems at Shakespeare's Globe, the Southbank Centre and the Cheltenham Literature Festival among others, and she loves running workshops in primary schools. Kate also writes for adults and a pamphlet of her poetry, *The Rainbow Faults*, is published by The Rialto. She lives in Oxford.

EILIDH MULDOON

grew up on the Scottish coast at North Berwick, and has an MFA in Illustration from Edinburgh College of Art, where she now teaches part-time in the illustration department. She was artist in residence at the Edinburgh International Book Festival in 2019, and the Fringe by the Sea Festival in 2021. She wrote and illustrated the picture book *Snooze!* and *An Art Adventure around the National Galleries of Scotland*. She runs frequent illustration and book-making workshops in schools, and never goes anywhere without her sketchbook. She lives in a small village on the Scottish coast.